MW01603005

COMPANION PLANTING

For Beginners and Intermediates

Secrets to Growing Vegetables, Fruits and Herbs; Soil Improvement and Pest Control

by

James McAllen

Dell Publishing Press

DISCLAIMER AND PUBLISHING RIGHTS

CONTENTS

Disclaimer and Publishing Rights   **2**

Introduction   **7**

Companion Planting   **9**

Choosing Companion Plants   *10*

Vegetables   **14**

Growing Vegetables   *15*

Planting your Garden   **18**

Garden Organization   *21*

Fruits   **23**

3 Different Types of Fruits That Can Be Grown in a Pot   *23*
    Strawberries   24
    Blueberries   26
    Figs   28

Wild Plants   *30*

Winter Protection   *31*

Growing Your Own Berries and Fruits   *32*
    Site Selection   33
    Selecting Plants   34
    Buying Plants   35

How to Plant a Fruit Tree   *37*

Pollination   *38*

Growing Your Own Herbs   **40**

Basil   *41*

Chives   *42*

Coriander   *43*

Dill   *44*

Fennel   *45*

Mint   *46*

Parsley   *47*

Sage   *48*

Tarragon   *49*

Thyme   *50*

Harvesting Herbs   *51*

Gardening Methods   **52**

Growing More in Less Space   *52*
Raised Beds   53
Vertical Gardening   53

Other Gardening Methods   **57**

Intensive Planting   *57*
Interplanting   59
Double Digging   60
No Digging   61

Soil Preparation   **62**

Soil Types   *63*

Soil Texture   *64*

Testing Your Soil   *66*

Improving Your Soil   *67*
Soil pH   68

Pest and Disease Control   **70**

Organic Pest Control   *71*
Homemade Organic Pest Controls   72

Proven Organic Pest Controls   *74*

Vegetable & Fruit Harvest Guide   **75**

Apples   *75*

Asparagus   *76*

Beans   *78*

Snap Beans   *79*

Shell Beans   *79*

Dried Beans   *79*

Broccoli   *80*

Cabbage   *82*

Carrots   *83*

Cauliflower   *84*

Sweet Corn   *85*

Eggplant   *87*

Lettuce   *88*

Leaf Lettuce (Romaine)   *88*
  Head Lettuce   90

Melons   *91*
  Muskmelons (also called cantaloupe, rock
  melon)   91
  Honeydews   92
  Watermelons   93

Bulb Onions and Garlic   *94*
  Bulb Onions   95
  Garlic   95

Snow and Snap Peas   *96*

Pears   *98*

Peppers   *99*

Potatoes   *101*

Pumpkins and other Squash   *103*
   Pumpkins and Winter Squash   103
   Summer Squash and Zuccini   104

Tomatoes   *106*

Conclusion   **108**

About the Author   **109**

More Books from Dell Publishing Press **110**

INTRODUCTION

People often find that they like certain people, and not others. Certain associations with a person or group of persons that you like can actually *help* your overall growth. By the same token, associations with people that may be deemed as being "bad company" can actually *hurt* your overall growth.

It turns out that it's exactly the same way with plants. Certain plants, when paired together, can exist in perfect harmony and can help one another's growth. Certain other plants, when paired together, can produce a disharmonious situation where growth is impeded. Certain harmful insects, such as aphids and certain beetle types, can also be attracted to these bad pairings.

You can benefit *financially* by having the right groupings of plants together, so you can avoid the losses of having crops that don't produce properly. You can also save money by having beneficial pairings of plants that produce bountifully.

The trick, then, is knowing which pairings are desirable, and which ones are not. It involves looking through a lot of scientific research, and just simple trial-and-error, in some cases. And just simply listening to the experiences of generations of gardeners that have gone before them. Those experiences are readily available on the internet and, in certain occasions, through word of mouth. And a great many of them are available through this eBook.

COMPANION PLANTING

Companion planting not only works, it has proven itself to be smart gardening. If you study and research it, you will discover you can group certain plants together that encourage each other's growth, and help to attract the good insects and keep the bad ones out. It might be the aroma or odor of a plant that protects its neighbors from pests, or the plant's roots might secrete pest-deterring substances. On occasion, it might be both. Either way, companion planting is a very good thing.

History has shown us that the early European settlers planted corn and beans together, as they were shown to do so by Native Americans. The cornstalk provides a structure that the bean vines can then climb. This clever arrangement allows two crops to grow in the same space. Not only do the corn and beans grow well together, the beans will also attract beneficial insects. These insects will eat any pests that are drawn to the corn. Because beans are members of the legume family, they also release nitrogen in the soil, allowing any plants nearby to utilize it.

Another example of a symbiotic relationship is the combination of tomatoes and marigolds. This is thought to repel nematodes, which are harmful to plants. As the repellent builds in the soil over time, you have to plant the "smelly" marigold flowers with the tomatoes for a minimum of 1 to 2 years to get the full benefit. It is also thought that the strong odor of old-fashioned marigolds may help drive away certain insects, too; some of the newer mixed versions (hybrids) of this flower may lack the smell that the older versions had. Other options for companion planting with tomatoes include carrots and parsley.

CHOOSING COMPANION PLANTS

Basil is thought to increase the flavor of tomatoes while it repels both disease and insects. Basil also benefits planting with asparagus, oregano, and peppers, but don't plant it near sage.

Beet plants do well grown with onions, lettuce, brassicas, and bush beans. Plant garlic with beets to enhance the growth and flavor of the beet vegetable.

Borage is loaded with minerals and its flowers invite parasitic wasps and beneficial pollinators. It is thought to boost the pest and disease resistance of any plant growing beside the borage.

Brassicas (common scientific groupings of cruciferous vegetables are the Brassica oleracea: broccoli, Brussels sprouts, cabbage,cauliflower, collards, kale, and kohlrabi, and the Brassica rapa: Chinese cabbage and turnips) grow best when planted with potatoes, marigolds, nasturtiums, bush beans, beets, dill, and onions, but **do not** grow them near eggplant, peppers, tomatoes, or strawberries.

Carrots are happy around peas, onions, and lettuce. **Do not** plant them near tomatoes, which stunt the carrots' growth and they also **do not** like being grown by dill, brassicas, or potatoes.

Cucumbers are good neighbors to sunflowers, nasturtiums, marigolds, onions, corn, lettuce, peas, and beans, but **do not** grown them with or near potatoes. If you plant radishes in each cucumber hill, they are thought to be a repellent against, or at least confuse cucumber beetles; they also repel flea beetles. The radish plants must flower to attract beneficial insects.

Fennel should be planted only with dill, which is strong enough to stand up to it. Fennel plants exude a substance that inhibits the growth of all other nearby plants.

Lettuce does well near radishes, strawberries, onions, cukes, carrots, beets and beans. But, lettuce **does not** do well when grown near parsley or brassicas. Planting mint repels slugs from eating your lettuce.

Lovage is thought to improve the flavor and growth of whatever you plant near it.

Onions, along with other alliums like shallots, leeks, garlic, and chives protect a large number of plants including roses but **do not** plant them near asparagus, peas, or beans.

Parsley grows well with carrots, roses, asparagus, and tomatoes.

Peas and beans enhance growth in many plants including strawberries, radishes, lettuce, eggplant, cukes, corn, carrots, and brassicas. Allegedly summer savory repels bean beetles and improves flavor and growth in beans. **Do not** Grow onions with peas or beans because they stunt each other's growth.

Peppers, both hot and sweet, are good companions to onions and basil.

Tomato growth can be improved when you grow them with nasturtiums, marigolds, parsley, basil and onions. **Do not** plant tomatoes with brassicas because both plants will suffer. **Do not** plant tomatoes with potatoes because both are susceptible to late blight.

To have enough effect, companion plants have to be grown in adequate quantity. One lonely summer savory plant at the end of each row of beans **will not** be as effective as interspersing them along each side and throughout each row.

Learning what to plant in a vegetable garden, and how to take care of them so they produce a bountiful harvest, is actually not all that hard. With proper planning, you can enjoy the fruits of your labor from a beautiful garden. You can also do that without having to spend hours and hours tending it. If you plant a garden that has both vegetables and flowers, you have already combined natural companions. This can turn a piece of unattractive piece of soil into an attractive piece of landscape.

For example, carrots and onions are very good to plant together, because it's been observed that carrots drive off the onion fly, and onions drive off the carrot fly. They help each other because they keep the other's "predator", if you will, from coming around in the first place. It truly is a mutually beneficial arrangement, that has been carried over through the generations.

This link gives a useful chart in regards to choosing companion plants.

http://downloads.smilinggardener.com/files/images/articles/vegetables/companion-planting-chart.pdf

As an example, start on the left side of the chart. Let's start with cabbage. Go across that row until it intersects the vertical row of "beans", at the top. The "smiley face" indicates that beans and cabbage are good to plant together. They are "companion plants". The legend is in the upper left of the chart. "Smiley face" in the box means they are good to plant together. An "X" means that they are **not**. A ruler may be useful to understand the chart better. Now go a couple of inches or so over in that same row, to where the row for cabbage intersects with garlic. There is an "X" in that box. That means that cabbage and garlic are "antagonistic", or they are **not** good to plant together. To the right of the table is some more information going down. It tells you what you can plant to help deter unwanted insects.

VEGETABLES

Picture of vegetables at a supermarket. Picture courtesy of Wikimedia. This image was originally posted to Flickr by Muffet at http://flickr.com/photos/53133240@N00/4206360542. It was reviewed on 2 September 2011 by the FlickreviewR robot and was confirmed to be licensed under the terms of the cc-by-2.0. User was Ahura21, and was submitted on 2 September 2011. Used under the Creative Commons Attribution 2.0 Generic license.

GROWING VEGETABLES

Image courtesy of Wikimedia.
A scanned red tomato, along with leaves and flowers.

Attributed to: David Besa from Sonoma, USA (Flickr) [CC BY 2.0 (http://creativecommons.org/licenses/by/2.0)], via Wikimedia Commons

If you are growing vegetables from seed, start your seeds 6-8 weeks before the last frost date in your area, indoors for best results. March is a good time to start pepper and tomato seeds, as it allows these late spring plants to get a head start on their growth. If you are growing a frost-hardy crop, these can be direct seeded to the garden without having to be started indoors.

If you're new to gardening, it's better to start with something small, and see how it works for you, than to become overwhelmed by a large garden you feel you can't handle.

Here are some basic concepts you'll need to know to get started:

> How much sun exposure do you have? Vegetables are sun lovers, and will need 6 hours of sun at the very least, and prefer 8 hours of sun if possible.

> What soil do you have? Vegetables prefer loamy, well-drained soil. If you don't have the perfect soil, you can amend your soil with compost. This will give your soil better drainage as well as plenty of nutrients.

> Place your garden where your plants will not need to compete with existing plants for nutrients and sun. If your garden is close to your home, it will also deter wild animals that may want to eat your crops.

> Choose whether you want to have a tilled garden or a raised bed. Raised beds lower the strain associated with gardening, and allow vegetables to be grown at arm's length.

> ➢ Vegetables need a lot of water, at least 1 inch of water a week. Many articles are available online, for how much and when to water vegetables.

> ➢ You'll need some essential tools for your garden. Start with these: spade, hoe, hand weeder, wheelbarrow, soaking hose, and also some good gardening gloves to keep your hands from getting messed up.

> ➢ Examine seed catalogs and order from those. Try to do so early.

> ➢ Know about the frost dates for your area, if you live in a northern climate or more temperate area. The Farmer's Almanac is useful for finding your last frost dates.

PLANTING YOUR GARDEN

Raised bed of lettuce, tomatoes, 6 different types of basil, marigolds, zinnias, garlic chives, zucchini. Taken on 31 July 2007. Author: Srl. Photo courtesy of Wikimedia.

A suggestion for someone just starting out in gardening is to start with a size about 16 X 10 feet, and plant some crops in it that are easy to grow. A plot this size, if done like it is suggested below, can feed a family of four for a whole summer, with a little extra for canning or freezing, or just giving to your mom or the neighbor down the street. If you choose this size of garden, the plot should be 11 rows wide, with each row being 10 feet long. Make the rows run north and south so you can get as much sun for the garden as you can. Don't forget to create paths between your rows that will accommodate any equipment you need to bring into your garden.

Before planting any vegetables, loosen the soil in your intended garden space. Depending on how large your space is, you may choose to use a trowel and dig by hand, or use a tiller. Avoid stepping on freshly tilled soil, as this will compact the soil, reversing any effect your tilling has had. After the soil is tilled, water and let the soil rest for a few days to a week before planting.

When choosing a location, keep in mind any windy locations in your yard. If your yard is frequently windy, consider planting trees or otherwise creating a wind buffer for your garden. If there are low-lying areas that experience frost earlier in fall and later in the spring than the rest of your yard, avoid placing your garden there.

You will find that watering and other routine tasks for your garden are easier on a level site. But, if only sloping land is available, try to find a south- or southeast-facing slope to take as much advantage from the sun as you can, and plant in a way that the tallest plants do not shade the smallest plants.

Some vegetables are good for any garden, and may even yield more than one crop per season. Those include carrots, cabbage, spinach, turnips, beans, beets, kohlrabi, rutabagas, lettuce, and radishes. Consider which plants grow best together before choosing your crop, as certain combinations of plants are antagonistic, and will hinder each other's growth.

Sometimes, you have conditions that just don't lend themselves to growing vegetables. Perhaps your soil is too hard to dig, or you have trees that shade your yard most of the day. In this case, container gardening would be ideal. Use a large container and potting soil, and place the container in an area that receives six to eight hours of full sun a day. Even if your soil is perfect for vegetables, container gardening can eliminate animal pest problems and help you deal with soil-borne diseases.

If you are in a particularly cold climate, container gardening can help you get your plants started long before the ground is ready to work. You can then transplant any frost-sensitive plants into your garden after the frost has passed.

Choosing decorative containers can lead to a beautiful container garden. Get some smaller pots to fill with flowers, and place those pots around your large vegetable pots. This creates a functional and beautiful garden.

You will find that starting a vegetable garden at home is indeed a good way to save money. Fresh vegetables are worth so much more than the initial cost,. There is nothing quite like having a fresh tomato straight from the plant. Grocery stores do try to provide good vegetables, but the freshest produce is always the produce you grow and pick yourself. Your garden can also become a peaceful retreat from responsibility and stress.

The practice of companion planting maintains the theory that certain plants can either inhibit, or in better cases enhance, the growth of other plants.

Researchers have discovered that this type of interplanting is beneficial in several ways. There are plants that repel or rather confuse insects; there are other plants that act like a magnet toward beneficial insects that either help pollination or are aggressive toward the harmful bugs. Still other plants provide more nutrients to the soil and that affects the flavor and growth of their companions or sometimes just provide shade to certain plants.

Three Sisters is a term long used by Native Americans in referring to the companion plant grouping of squash, pumpkins, corn and pole beans. Corn stalks shade pumpkin or squash plants whose prickly vines smother weeds and even discourage animals from trying to feast on the beans and corn. While using the cornstalks for support, pole bean plants return nitrogen that corn plants consume. Below are how more companion plants work.

GARDEN ORGANIZATION

Typically, most vegetables are grown in rows separated by paths that give you access to the plants, so you can till or hoe the soil. This plan works best for plants that grow very tall (such as corn) and for those plants that need support, such as pole beans and tomatoes. A kind of garden that may be familiar to you is the Three Sisters garden, which makes use of hill planting. Hill planting means that seeds or plants are grouped in a cluster, but not necessarily on a mound. For wide sprawling plants, such as some kinds of squash, hills can be very useful.

Many vegetables of the smaller variety, such as spinach, carrots, beets, and lettuce, can be grown more efficiently using the wide bed arrangement. In this setup, you prepare a bed using a width of about 3 feet, then broadcast the seeds over it (i.e., sprinkle the seeds around) rather than planting them in rows.

Paths on either side of the plants allow for good access to them. However, you'll waste much less space on paths than you would in a row-planting plan. The benefit of this is that it gives you more room for vegetables.

FRUITS

3 DIFFERENT TYPES OF FRUITS THAT CAN BE GROWN IN A POT

While some would consider luxury to be an pricey car or designer clothing, the luxury of fresh fruit is something everyone can have. Even if you don't have hundreds to invest in gardens or 8 hours a day to devote to your plants, it is still possible to produce delicious fruit. Pot gardening is especially useful for those who have little experience or can't maintain a garden in the ground.

If you choose to container garden, your plants will need more frequent watering and possibly more fertilizer, as they are unable to reach out with their roots to collect natural nutrients or water. Using a drip irrigation system on a timer may give you more freedom, allowing plants to receive water even when you cannot be there to supply it. Additionally, winter conditions are harsher on plants in containers, so protecting these plants will become a priority as the weather becomes colder.

These three plants are great candidates for pot gardening, as they adapt well to confined spaces and are hardy enough for even the most amateur gardener.

STRAWBERRIES

Strawberries are ideal for anyone who wants a huge summer crop of delicious fruit. Depending on your schedule, you can choose June-bearers, ever-bearers, day-neutrals, or alpine berries. If you are looking to turn your berries into jam or use your entire crop within a few days, June-bearers are a good option. The berries will ripen all at once, giving plenty of fruit for preserving or feeding a huge crowd. Don't choose a June-bearing variety if you want to enjoy your fruit over time, as you'll lose a lot of good fruit it goes bad.

Ever-bearers have two crops, one in June, and another later in the summer. While not as ideal for preserving, it does spread the harvest further. Day-neutrals are the ultimate for anyone who wants to run out and pick a fresh berry anytime in the summer. They produce smaller berries, but they produce all summer and don't require as much commitment as a larger single harvest would require. Alpine berries are very small and require little maintenance, and the fruits are very fragrant. These are best for window boxes, as the fruits are more decorative than anything else. While they are perennials, strawberries tend to live only 2 to 3 years before their useful life is up. Once your harvests decline, buy fresh plants and replant using fresh soil.

Pot: Two 18-inch containers should be plenty of room for a 25 plant bunch. The containers can be as shallow as 10 inches deep; strawberries do not require deep soil.

Soil: Strawberries hate wet feet, and will rot if kept wet. They enjoy light, rich soil, with a ratio of 1 part compost to 3 parts potting mix.

Light: Your strawberry containers should be receiving 8 hours of direct sun or more per day. Good airflow is a must, as it will prevent fungal diseases.

Water: While overwatering will cause your strawberries to rot, they do require frequent watering, as their roots are shallow.

Varieties: For container gardening, day-neutral or alpine berry varieties are ideal. Ever-bearers are also an option if your climate is particularly hot. Choose a variety based on your goals in growing and desired taste/size.

Pruning: Prune runners unless you are interested in propagating your plants.

Fertilizer: Strawberries should receive a low-nitrogen fertilizer three times a year. Fertilize in early spring when you begin to plant, again after the last frost has passed, and midway through the summer.

Hardiness: Strawberries may thrive in USDA Plant Hardiness Zones 3-9, but some varieties are hardier than others.

BLUEBERRIES

Blueberries thrive in containers, and are actually better grown that way if your soil is alkaline; they love acidic soil (between 4.5 and 5.5). While the berries ripen from late June to August, the plant is beautiful throughout the seasons. The plants have bell-shaped flowers in the spring, fruits in late summer, autumn colors, and even during winter, bright red stems. Blueberries may be a problem for gardeners with a small space requirement, as many varieties need two plants for good fruit.

Pot: Blueberry plants live long lives and need room for large root systems, so plan ahead and get a large container that is at least 18 inches deep with a 22-inch diameter.

Soil: Blueberries like peat-based potting mixes, as they tend to give the acidic conditions that blueberries love so much. Blending sphagnum peat moss 50/50 with compost gives the perfect soil combination.

Light: Blueberries will need at least 6 hours of full sun per day.

Water: Blueberries love frequent watering, especially in summer, when they need it for fruit. But even out of season, do water your blueberries often.

Recommended varieties: Select varieties that do well in your climate. There are also dwarf varieties available for gardeners with space limitations.

Pruning: Early spring is the best time to prune blueberry plants. Prune branches that are about three years old, as this promotes new growth, and the new growth will bear more fruit than the old growth. After harvest, you can prune again to shape your plants, but only lightly.

Fertilizer: There are special fertilizers available for woody acid lovers like blueberries, in granular form. Fertilize twice a year, once in early spring and once in early June, before the fruit ripens.

Hardiness: Blueberries have been known to thrive in USDA Plant Hardiness Zones 2-8. If in a colder climate, choose a cold-hardy variety.

FIGS

While the Mediterranean style of a fig tree is great for decorating, if your area gets any sort of frost during winter, your figs need to be in containers for their own protection. Container figs also make it easy for you to move the plant to a spot warm enough to ripen the fruits, as they require plenty of warmth to produce good fruit. A south-facing wall is a great spot for these sun lovers. But don't forget to move the plant inside as soon as it gets cold, as the buds are very sensitive to cold. All but a few varieties will produce two crops, the smaller harvest on the previous year's growth, and the larger harvest on new growth.

Pot: While figs can become very large if given the room, containers direct the plant to produce more fruit rather than grow to full size. When looking for a pot, choose one at least 16 inches across and deep, larger if your variety needs more space.

Soil: Fig trees like well-drained soil, but aren't picky otherwise. A 50/50 ratio of potting mix to compost is fine for your figs.

Light: For the fruit to ripen, figs require full sun, and a lot of it. Place your figs where they will receive tons of light in the summer, and bring them inside to protect them from frost.

Water: Figs are drought-hardy, but because of their light needs, will need frequent watering. If you are unable to water as much as the tree needs, you can mulch the plant or set up a drip system so they receive the water they need to produce fruit.

Varieties: Choose a variety based on your climate; some varieties are more cold tolerant than others.

Pruning: If you are keeping your figs in containers, try to limit their growth to 6 feet. Letting them grow further means less ability to prune in the future, or pick the fruits. It's better to just shorten the stems rather than remove them, as there will be buds remaining for the next early crop.

Fertilizer: Fertilize figs cautiously, as over fertilizing will just make the plant grow more branches and divert away from fruit production. Top-dressing with compost and a woody plant fertilizer each spring will be plenty.

Hardiness: Depending on your variety, the tree may be able to withstand winters in Zones 5-7 with protection. It is better to move your fig to a place where it is cool, but there is no freezing, but if your fig is in the ground, you can wrap the plant and limit any damage from frost.

WILD PLANTS

Wild red raspberry bush about a few weeks before the raspberries become pickable and edible. In Bloomingdale, New Jersey. Photo courtesy of Wikimedia. Taken on 8 June 2012. Author: Tomwsulcer. This file is made available under the Creative Commons CC0 1.0 Universal Public Domain Dedication.

When planning a garden, one thing you should consider is choosing plants native to your area. While those exotics may be beautiful, plants from your area are better adapted to survive in your garden and likely enjoy the natural soil, reducing the need for soil amendments. Wildlife in your area will also benefit from your native plants, as the nectar, pollen and seeds are the best food for the local butterflies, birds, and other animals. There are also likely to be beneficial bugs in your area that will find your plants and reduce or eliminate the need for pesticides.

WINTER PROTECTION

When container gardening, always consider that your plants do not have as much soil to protect their roots. Try to choose a variety that thrives in a full zone lower than yours, to ensure that they are not killed by the cold. If overwintering your plants outside, try to protect them from wind and direct sunlight; placing the containers near a wall may help to protect them.

Another option to protect your plants' roots is to create a hill of mulch, compost, or soil around the pot, up to the pot's rim. Strawberry crowns are especially delicate, so remember to insulate them with dry straw. 2 or 3 inches of straw will protect the crowns from the cold. Whenever the soil is not frozen, ensure that your dormant plants have moisture.

GROWING YOUR OWN BERRIES AND FRUITS

Image courtesy of Wikipedia. Photograph of an apple tree. Taken on 24 October 2007.Author: Aomorikuma. Permission is granted to copy, distribute and/or modify this document under the terms of the GNU Free Documentation License, Version 1.2 or any later version published by the Free Software Foundation; with no Invariant Sections, no Front-Cover Texts, and no Back-Cover Texts. A copy of the license is included in the section entitled GNU Free Documentation License.

Even if you don't have the space for a big orchard, you can still produce your own fruits by planting your own trees. For those with space limits, there are dwarf versions of pears, apples, and other delicious fruits. You can also train a tree to a wall or trellis by using the technique called espalier. Some varieties can even be planted in a container, giving even more control over the space the plant occupies.

SITE SELECTION

Fruiting trees are picky about their location, but for a home orchard, the best you can do is pick the most ideal location on your land and hope for the best.

Soil: Loamy, well-drained soil is ideal for fruit trees, as they hate wet feet. There should also be ample air circulation, as fungus will grow on the leaves if they are allowed to remain wet.

Frost: Avoid planting your trees in a frost pocket or in a particularly windy place, as this will cause the flower buds to die from frost. If your land is sloped, plant your trees in the middle of the slope, as the bottom of the slope will be prone to frost, and the top of the slope will be the windiest location.

Slope direction: It is usually best to avoid slopes if possible. If you are forced to plant your trees on a slope, you have to compare the downsides of each direction of slope. Northern slopes will allow the trees to remain dormant past the late frosts, but the trees may not get enough sun to evaporate any moisture, or to allow fruits to ripen properly. Eastern slopes will give the most sun in the morning, and will help dry the dew from the leaves, but leave the plants with less sun in the afternoon.

While southern slopes receive the most sun, the trees may break dormancy before it is time, leaving them vulnerable to late frosts. Southern slopes will work best if there is a windbreak somewhere except for the bottom of the slope.

Sun: Always try to place your plants in full sun, as this will give them the best conditions for fruit production, as well as deterring both insects and disease.

SELECTING PLANTS

Disease should always be a consideration when choosing a variety, as well as choosing your actual plants. Many varieties are resistant to one or more diseases, and these varieties should be high on your list when choosing your variety. Regardless of whether your variety is resistant or not, always check to make sure your plant is free of disease. If the nursery has multiple plants that have some form of disease, it is probably not a good idea to choose even a healthy plant from this nursery, as your plant may carry a disease, but not show it. While you may still have issues with disease, choosing healthy plants will limit your chance of having disease occur in your garden.

When choosing a variety, one of your main concerns should be hardiness. The hardiest varieties are often the best, especially if you are new to gardening or live in an area that has harsh winters. Many fruit bearing plants will flower early, and late frosts will kill off your flowers, so you never see fruit. The plant may survive, but it'll just be a leafy plant and not produce. If you live in a warm, humid area, choosing a heat hardy plant will make it easier for you to care for your plants.

BUYING PLANTS

Depending on where you purchase your plants, you will either have a bareroot stock, a dormant plant with the roots packed in slightly damp shavings, or a container grown sapling. Some places will wrap the roots of their plants in burlap.

Mail order nurseries will usually have more varieties, but they will almost always have bare root stock. These varieties may or may not be suited to your area, so a local nursery may be a better place to start if you are looking for a plant that will thrive in your garden.

If you choose to purchase bare root stock, you should purchase them in the winter and plant once the ground is thawed enough to work. Planting early gives the new trees a chance to put down roots and send out new growth before the winter comes again.

If your plant is in a container, the container is likely too small for the plant even at its current size. Purchase a larger container if you intend to have a container garden. If you intend to transplant the tree into your garden or other suitable location, choose between a fall planting and a spring planting. Planting in the fall means the plant will be dormant for a longer time, but this should be fine.

Wherever you choose to buy from, the tree you buy will likely have been grafted. This graft allows the tree to produce the exact variety of fruit you desire, but part of the tree will be of a different variety, sometimes resulting in two kinds of fruit on the same tree. Often, the graft is from a full size tree, and the rootstock is from a dwarf tree, allowing a full size variety to be produced with a dwarf size plant. Some rootstocks are semi-dwarfing, giving a full size between 8 feet and 15 feet.

Dwarf trees are likely the most desirable for your garden, as they are space efficient and bear fruit quickly. However, they don't live as long as a normal tree (10 to 20 years) and don't do well when forced to compete for space with other plants. Keep the ground around your tree's root system mulched and weeded, or your tree will struggle to compete with the wild plants. Dwarf varieties also do best in mild climates, as they are not as cold hardy as a full size tree. If you live in an area with a harsh winter, you will probably need to devote the space to a full size tree.

HOW TO PLANT A FRUIT TREE

For bare root nursery stock, the roots should be soaked in water or manure tea for several hours (up to 24) before planting. If the ground is still too cold to work, keep the plant in the wood shavings it was packaged in, and allow the plant to remain dormant in a cold, dark location until you can plant. Do not let the plant be exposed to wind or sun.

After you have a good planting location, dig a circle 2 feet in diameter and roughly 3 feet deep with your spade. Set the sod aside. Separate the topsoil and subsoil, and remove any rocks from the site. Place the sod in the hole, grass side down. Cover the sod with topsoil.

Gently set your tree into the hole. If you have a grafted tree, the graft should be 1 to 2 inches below the ground. If you have a dwarf tree, the graft should be 2 to 3 inches above the ground. Fill in the hole about halfway, using your topsoil first. Make sure the soil is firm and that there are no air pockets. Water thoroughly, until the soil is quite muddy. Press the soil down again with your foot.

Continue filling in the hole, and make a depression around the tree so that any water will drain toward the tree. Again, make sure the soil is pressed down. Place mulch around the tree. This can be any organic material, but do not use fresh manure. The mulch should follow the depression around the tree. Once you have finished mulching, water the tree until the soil will not hold any more water.

Stake the tree into the ground. The stakes should be outside the root zone. After staking, prune side branches and cut back the branches by about a third. If the tree was balled or in a container, it will not need pruning. To deter deer and rodents, put a tree guard on your tree.

Throughout the first growing season, water the tree with about 5 to 10 gallons a day for the first month, and then gradually backing off on the water through the next few months, especially when the tree has been watered by rainfall. During late fall, paint the bark with white latex paint (diluted with water). This will make the bark reflect any sun and prevents cracking.

POLLINATION

Even if you choose a plant that self-pollinates, your plants will likely still benefit from having another plant close by of a different variety. Some varieties require another variety close by to produce any good fruit at all. Cross pollination doesn't create hybrid fruits, only seeds that are not true to type. If you have a specific variety, it will always produce that variety's fruits, even if it is pollinated with a different variety's pollen. But if you plant the seed from your own plants, it will grow different apples than your original tree. Cross pollination makes your trees bear more fruit, albeit ones that carry a different seed.

While commercial orchards are usually pollinated by rented honeybee hives, your wild bees will likely pollinate your plants without any encouragement. Just don't spray any pesticides while your plants (or any wild plants near them) are blooming. You'll accidentally kill your pollinators. If you must kill pests during pollination time, use a nonchemical method, so you don't kill any of your bees or other beneficial bugs.

GROWING YOUR OWN HERBS

Herbs usually don't need as much sun as your vegetables and fruits, but place them in a location that will get at least 4 hours of sun a day, preferably more. Herbs do work well in pots, but be sure to place them in a window or close to one.

Photograph courtesy of Wikimedia. This image, which was originally posted to Flickr.com, was uploaded to Commons using Flickr upload bot on 15:19, 22 August 2012 (UTC) by Darwinius. This file is licensed under the Creative Commons Attribution 2.0 Generic license. Taken: 26 November 2010|Author: Alexander Baxevanis. Description: At Mercado dos Lavradores, Funchal.

BASIL

Photo courtesy of Wikimedia. This file is licensed under the Creative Commons Attribution-Share Alike 3.0 Unported, 2.5 Generic, 2.0 Generic and 1.0 Generic licenses. By Castielli.

Basil leaves have a warm, spicy flavor. Basil is a classic spice, used in dishes ranging from salads to meat and soups. It is also used as a base for pesto.

When growing basil, start the seeds inside near a sunny window or in a greenhouse, before the last frost date. Once the last frost date has passed, transplant to your garden. You can also direct seed basil into your garden, but only after the frost has passed.

CHIVES

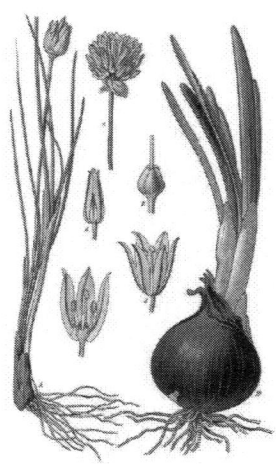

Picture courtesy of Wikimedia. This work is in the public domain in its country of origin and other countries and areas where the copyright term is the author's life plus 80 years or less.

Chives leaves have a very mild and pleasant onion flavor. They are a must have for salads, egg and cheese dishes, mashed potatoes, and sauces. The flowers are edible and can also be used in salads.

Chives are best sown directly in the garden, in spring or fall. Plant the seeds ½ inch deep, with rows about a foot apart. Once established, the rows should be thinned so the plants are 6 inches apart.

CORIANDER

Coriander (Coriandrum sativum) leaves. Photo courtesy of Wikimedia. Author: Thamizhpparithi Maari, taken on 31 December 2011. Used under the Creative Commons Attribution-Share Alike 3.0 Unported license.

Coriander can be grown for the leaves or for the seeds, or both. The leaves are referred to as cilantro, and is a common herb in Mexican dishes. The seeds can be ground and used to season meats. The roots are also edible, and are used to flavor soup. Coriander will attract bees into your garden, and is a great option for companion planting, as carrots and cabbage pests hate coriander plants.

Coriander seeds should be direct sown into the garden, ¼ inches deep, with rows a foot apart. Thin once the seedlings are established, to 6 inches apart.

DILL

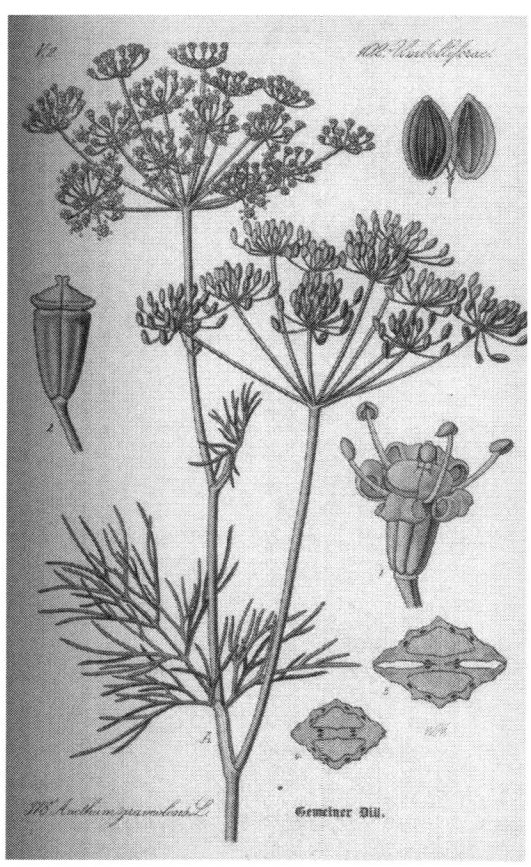

Photo courtesy of Wikimedia. This work is in the public domain in its country of origin and other countries and areas where the copyright term is the author's life plus 80 years or less.

Dill has a very distinct, sharp flavor. While dill seed does have this flavor, the leaves are the most commonly used. Dill is very versatile and is used to flavor a variety of dishes, as well as having a use in pickling.

Direct sow dill seeds in rows 9 inches apart, about ¼ inch deep. Thin seedlings to 9 inches apart.

FENNEL

Photo courtesy of Wikimedia. Attribution to Arnaud 25 (Own work) [Public domain], via Wikimedia Commons

Fennel should be sown in groups of 3 to 4 seeds in mid-spring. These groups should be spaced 18 inches apart and ¼ inch deep. The strongest seedling should be left to grow, and the other seedlings should be thinned.

MINT

Photo courtesy of Wikimedia. Author: Kham Tran, taken on 10 November 2007. Permission is granted to copy, distribute and/or modify this document under the terms of the GNU Free Documentation License, Version 1.2 or any later version published by the Free Software Foundation; with no Invariant Sections, no Front-Cover Texts, and no Back-Cover Texts. A copy of the license is included in the section entitled GNU Free Documentation License.

Mint is a common, hardy herb often used in tea or candies. It can also be used to season lamb, but the most common use of fresh mint is for mint tea.

Mint can be planted in autumn or spring. To start a mint plant, you can acquire a piece of root about 4 to 6 inches long and bury it 2 inches deep, watering well. The plant will regrow from the root. Mint likes to take over areas and never leave, so put boards or bricks 1 foot deep around any mint beds. Alternately, you can plant the mint in a plastic bucket that has the bottom cut out and has been sunk into the garden bed. While it's unlikely you'll ever need more than one plant, as they grow like crazy, there should be 12 inches of space between the mint and any other plant, as well as that barrier.

PARSLEY

Photo courtesy of Wikimedia. Parsley in a greenhouse. Date of photo: 9 July 2005 (according to Exif data). The work is released into the public domain.

Parsley can be used in salads, soups, stews, or casseroles, but is also used as a garnish for various other dishes.

Your planting time will depend on when you want to harvest the parsley. Mid-spring is best for a summer harvest, while midsummer is best if you want to harvest in autumn or winter. Parsley seeds should be soaked overnight and then direct sown into the garden. Seedlings should be thinned to 9 or 10 inches apart.

SAGE

Photograph courtesy of Wikipedia. Author: Jonathunder. Photograph taken on 8 August 2013. Permission is granted to copy, distribute and/or modify this document under the terms of the GNU Free Documentation License, Version 1.2 only as published by the Free Software Foundation; with no Invariant Sections, no Front-Cover Texts, and no Back-Cover Texts.

Dried sage leaves are great for seasoning lamb, pork, and sausage. They are also traditionally used in poultry stuffing.

If you are direct seeding, sow in early spring. If using nursery grown plants, plant them in your garden in mid-spring, with about 1 foot between the plants.

TARRAGON

Image courtesy of Wikimedia. This work has been released into the public domain by its author, KVDP at English Wikipedia. This applies worldwide. KVDP grants anyone the right to use this work for any purpose, without any conditions, unless such conditions are required by law.

Tarragon leaves are used to season soups, salads, stews, and lamb. They are also used to season butter for use with fish, steak, or vegetables. Tarragon is essential to making tartar sauce and several chutneys.

Tarragon does not grow true from seed, so you will need to find nursery grown plants to have your own tarragon plant. The nursery plants will need to be set out in early spring, about 18 inches apart.

THYME

Image courtesy of Wikimedia. Flowering thyme. Author: Greenmars. Photograph taken on 19 May 2013. Source: Own work. This file is licensed under the Creative Commons Attribution-Share Alike 3.0 Unported license.

Chopped thyme leaves can be rubbed onto meats such as lamb veal, or beef before roasting to infuse flavor. Thyme is also great with eggs, fish, rice, poultry, vegetables and soups. When mixed with rosemary and mint, thyme also makes a good tea.

Plant thyme seeds in shallow rows, about 1 foot apart, in mid-spring. Thin seedlings to 6 inches apart. If using nursery grown plants, set them out in early spring about 6 to 9 inches apart.

HARVESTING HERBS

To harvest herbs:

1. Cut the entire branches.

2. Rinse gently in cool water.

3. Hang upside down in small bunches.

4. In 2 - 3 weeks, remove the leaves and place in an air-tight container.

5. Grind or crush before using.

GARDENING METHODS

Following are several different ways you can grow your garden.

GROWING MORE IN LESS SPACE

Raised bed garden. Photograph courtesy of Wikimedia. Author: B. Blechmann. Taken during the summer of 2006. Permission is granted to copy, distribute and/or modify this document under the terms of the GNU Free Documentation License, Version 1.2 or any later version published by the Free Software Foundation; with no Invariant

Sections, no Front-Cover Texts, and no Back-Cover Texts.

RAISED BEDS

Raised beds involve raising the level of the garden's soil higher than the ground level. When working a raised bed, you can change the soil conditions easily, giving your raised bed fluffier and richer soil than your normal soil. This gives your plants easy access to any nutrients. You also don't have to bend over to till your garden, as the plants are right within arm's reach. When creating raised beds, the bed should not be wider than you can reach. If you have access to both sides, make sure you can reach halfway into the bed from each side.

VERTICAL GARDENING

Vertical gardens make use of many plants' tendency to take up a lot of space, by training the plants to grow upward rather than letting them sprawl and take up all of your gardening space. Fences and trellises with plants trained to them can provide shade for your patio or create a privacy barrier. There are many other options besides fences and trellises, including hanging baskets, cages, poles with netting attached, or arbors.

While many plants can be trained to grow on a support, some plants just won't work well with a vertical garden. You can still incorporate those plants as ground cover for your garden, though.

Plants that grow in a vertical garden:

1 Tomatoes do best when grown vertically than if they are left on the ground. Tomatoes are especially prone to disease when left to sprawl, and a sprawling tomato plant can easily outgrow any space. Cages are the most ideal vertical arrangement for tomato plants.

2. Cucumbers are naturally a great choice for vertical gardens. Their vines can be trained easily to your chosen support system.

3. As a straight-growing plant, corn can be used as a living support for peas, beans, and other climbing plants.

4. Other plants that can be easily trained to grow upwards are melons, passion fruit, zucchinis, pumpkins, and other various squashes. These will usually require good support to grow upwards, but especially in the case of pumpkins, it may be very impractical to let them sprawl. When trained to grow upwards, squashes and other sprawling plants become much more space efficient.

TIPS FOR A SUCCESSFUL VERTICAL GARDEN

1. Vertically grown plants will usually get plenty of sun, but don't forget about your ground plants. They may get shaded out by the climbing plants.

2. If you are growing your plants on a wall, plant them on a south wall so they will get the most sun possible. Water frequently, especially if you don't have any ground cover; the soil will dry out fast.

3. Well drained, fluffy soil is an absolute must for vertical gardens, as otherwise your plants will grow outward underneath the soil and will take up much more space than intended, crowding your other plants.

4. If growing melons, pumpkins, squash, or any other heavy crop, support the fruit as it grows. Otherwise, gravity will take over and your fruit will fall to the ground, likely making a mess.

OTHER GARDENING METHODS

INTENSIVE PLANTING

Whether you have a raised bed or a large garden in your yard, intensive gardening can maximize your garden's production by using every bit of space possible. Usually there is less weeding, involved since plants are spaced closer together, and every bit of garden space is cultivated throughout the entire growing season. The drawbacks are that you can't use machinery, as the plants are just too close together. Any weeding necessary will have to be done by hand. Additionally, there won't be a specific harvest time, as you will always have some plants still growing and some ready to harvest.

Intensive gardening uses space as efficiently as possible, as there are no wasted areas between rows of crops. The standard garden has straight, long rows of vegetables, with wide rows to accommodate wheelbarrows and other machinery. Much of the garden area is taken by the space between the rows, and is unable to be used for other plants. An intensive garden eliminates that waste by populating every possible inch of the garden.

Raised beds are excellent candidates for intensive planting. The raised beds do well because the soil amendments are concentrated in the bed only, so little fertilizer is wasted. The soil also warms faster, allowing vegetables to be planted sooner. The main concern with an intensively planted raised bed is water; you may want to set up a drip system so you aren't the only source of water through the hot summer months.

If you're considering an intensive garden, think about whether you want neat, straight rows, or a garden that is so full of plants, you think it could be a jungle. The neat, straight rows are conductive to machine weeding, but the intensive garden will not be. If you think that the relatively low weed amounts and constant harvest is good for you, then you may want to try an intensive garden.

Always consider companion planting when planning an intensive garden. Planting incompatible plants together could be disastrous. Consider planting herbs in the smaller spaces, rather than try to crowd larger plants all together in the same area. These herbs may also ward off pests, allowing your vegetables to grow freely.

INTERPLANTING

Interplanting is a method of gardening that involves growing two or more plants together. This is often done by gardeners who wish to companion plant. Interplanting can be done by alternating rows in a bed, alternating plants within a row, or just mixing plants together.

Even if you are not companion planting, consider what your plants need to thrive and plant similar plants together. If you plant the wrong plants together, they could shade out the other plants or even have allelopathic effects, in the case of sunflowers and Jerusalem artichokes. Different plants also like different soils, so if you plant a variety that loves acidic soil with one who loves alkaline soil, neither will thrive. Those plants would be much happier apart. Whereas, if you plant an herb that drives away pests next to your vegetable plants, you'll have much healthier and happier plants.

DOUBLE DIGGING

Double digging involves digging your beds to two spades deep, so the lower layer of soil is brought to the surface. The thought behind this is that it creates air pockets in the soil and breaks up any big clumps that your plants may struggle with. Critics of the double dig method say that it is pointless to dig so deep, as there are no nutrients in the lower soil.

Another point is that many plants have shallow root systems and do not require their soil loosened down to the two spade depth. If you have plants that require loose, fertile soil deep in the ground, double digging may be good for you, but otherwise, only one spade depth would be plenty. If you choose to dig over the winter, leave it roughly dug, as the frost will lend a hand in breaking up clumps. After the winter passes, you can rake to create nice, fine beds.

NO DIGGING

Some gardeners prefer to avoid digging in their beds at all, as they believe it is only the very top of the soil that needs to be worked. They also do not want to disrupt their soil structure with any digging. These gardeners will dig a bed initially, but leave it from that point on, only raking the top layer of soil and adding compost there. This method may work best if you don't have the time or energy to dig, or simply want to leave the soil as it is.

SOIL PREPARATION

Soil preparation is essential to any gardening style. Vegetables are delicate, and they require light, rich soil to produce good food. If the soil is hard and infertile, they will not thrive, and your garden will be a failure. The best way to enrich your soil is to add compost. The natural material will encourage earthworms to come to your garden, and they will create air pockets for your vegetables.

If your soil is not soft deeper down, digging your beds may be the best way to aerate the soil and get amendments deeper down. First, remove the first foot of soil. Insert your spade fully into the soil, and just wiggle your spade to break up any compaction. Repeat this every 6 to 8 inches. You can then mix the topsoil with compost, and return it to the bed. This should give plenty of air and nutrients to the soil, and draw earthworms to keep the air pockets.

If you're feeling overwhelmed, remember to start small. While you may need several beds dug for all the plants you want to grow, you can do one a day. Just make sure not to step on the beds you've already dug. It will undo all your hard work.

SOIL TYPES

Photo courtesy of Wikimedia. Author: Thamizhpparithi Maari. Taken: 22 December 2011. Description: A red soil crop field in Salem. This file is licensed under the Creative Commons Attribution-Share Alike 3.0 Unported license.

Soil type will largely decide what vegetables you can grow, as plants that need different conditions will not thrive in your garden. Finding out your soil texture and pH is important, but remember to test all over your garden, as it can vary throughout your plot.

SOIL TEXTURE

Soil is composed of three kinds of sediment: clay, silt, and sand. Ideally, your soil would have almost equal proportions of each, which is called loamy soil. This soil is naturally fertile and well-drained, and is very easy to dig. It's not likely that you'll have perfect loamy soil, so you will need to choose plants based on your soil combination and how much you can improve the soil with amendments.

Sandy soil is well-draining due to gaps between the large, gritty particles. However, sandy soil does not hold fertility well, as the nutrients will drain away with the water. If your soil tends to be sandy, you will need to water more frequently, as the soil will dry quickly. The upside to having sandy soil is that the soil will warm quickly and will be easier to dig than clay-based soil.

When choosing plants for sandy soil, consider choosing root vegetables and drought-hardy plants. Root vegetables will be able to easily push through the sandy soil and reach water beneath the surface, and drought-hardy plants will resist any dryness caused by the sand.

Photograph courtesy of Wikimedia Commons. This file is licensed under the Creative Commons Attribution-Share Alike 3.0 Unported license. Description: Typical soil found in Auroville, Tamil Nadu, India. Very rich in clay. Author: Carla Antonini. Photograph taken: 30 June 2012.

The heavier soils are silt and clay. Of the two, you would be much better off having a silt soil, as clay is extremely hard to dig and will be heavy even when dry. Both silt and clay will retain water and nutrients much better than sandy soil, but can become waterlogged. This can cause your plants to rot, especially if your plant is vulnerable to rot. These heavier soils will retain nutrients, but may take a long time to warm up in the spring. For both clay and silt soils, brassicas will grow better than root vegetables, and shallow-rooted plants and trees will thrive, as it holds moisture well.

If you have high clay soil, raised beds are highly recommended. Purchase soil that is light and fluffy, and amend the soil above the ground level. Your plants will not be able to push through that heavy clay. In the case that you have no other option and must garden with high clay soil, you should try to mix as much compost in as possible, and consider buying soil to mix into the clay and lighten it.

It is always important to create good paths through your garden, as walking will compact the soil, regardless of what type you have.

TESTING YOUR SOIL

To find out what kind of soil you have, make a ball of damp (not fully wet) soil between your hands and feel the texture.

If your soil is gritty and sticky, it is loam. This is the ideal soil for growing crops.

If the soil forms a ball easily and feels rough to the touch, it is clay loam.

If the soil forms a ball easily, becomes shiny when smoothed, and is somewhat gritty, it is a sandy clay.

If the soil forms a ball easily, becomes shiny when smoothed, and is not gritty, it is clay.

If the soil forms a ball easily but the ball is easily broken, it is loamy sand.

If the soil will not form a ball well and is gritty, it is sand.

If the soil is silky and slippery, it is silty loam.

IMPROVING YOUR SOIL

Organic materials (leaf mold and compost) are essential to the gardener. These will add nutrients to the soil and improve water drainage, as well as breaking up soils with high clay content and helping sandy soil to retain water and nutrients.

Most gardeners will not need to add organic materials more than once a year, but in some cases, it may be necessary.

Photograph courtesy of Wikimedia. Description: Analysing samples using Nitrogen Analyser. Author: Balaji Kasirajan. Date taken: 24 October 2010. This file is licensed under the Creative Commons Attribution-Share Alike 3.0 Unported license.

SOIL PH

pH is a measure of your soil's acidity or alkalinity. If your soil has a pH lower than 7, it is acidic; if your soil has a pH higher than 7, it is alkaline. If you've tried gardening in the past without much success, your soil's pH could be the cause. Some vegetables prefer acidic soil, while others prefer alkaline soil. In the case that you want to grow a specific vegetable that needs a soil pH you don't have, you may be able to create those soil conditions in a pot. In some cases, you may be able to add a soil amendment to create the pH you need to grow a certain plant in the ground. For example, adding lime to the soil before planting brassicas allows them to thrive in the alkalinity and even prevents disease.

Most plants grow best in soil with a pH of between 6.5 and 6.8, save a few. You can identify the soil's pH using a testing kit. These vary in pricing, but the more expensive kids usually provide more reliable results. Because pH can vary throughout your plot, take small samples from different areas. Avoid taking wet soil in your samples. Place each sample in a polythene bag and label it with where in the garden it came from. Allow your samples to dry, and then use your testing kit to determine the pH. Once you know the pH of your garden, you can then pick vegetables that suit your natural soil, and decide whether to pot some plants rather than try to grow them in un-ideal conditions.

PEST AND DISEASE CONTROL

It's very likely that you will struggle with plant diseases and pests in your garden at one point. While there are many chemicals available to fight pests, the chemicals may kill beneficial insects as well. Additionally, the chemicals may end up polluting your garden and your local water source. When choosing a method of pest control, consider choosing a natural or alternative method that will keep the pests off your crops, without killing your friendly bugs or the risk of accidental pollution.

Keep an eye on your plants to spot early signs of infestation. Many insects will be harmless, or even helpful, but identifying a pest early can give you a chance to pick them off before your crops are damaged.

Here are some tips to deal with pests in your garden:

While not every variety is resistant to disease, breeders have created some disease resistant varieties that naturally resist disease.

Damp conditions can lead to sick plants. If your plants are well spaced and given access to open air, this will combat rot and fungi. When watering, avoid getting water on the leaves. If the soil is too dry or wet, try to bring it back to a balance.

Plant different crops in the areas of your garden every year. If your plants were infested or ill last season, the pests or germs are likely still in that plot. Plant a different crop there that is not affected by that particular ailment.

As mentioned before, keep an eye on your plants. If you see diseased foliage or fruit, remove it. Pests can be removed by hand and put into soapy water before they cause any damage.

Washing your hands prevents the spread of disease, even plant diseases. Both before and after gardening, wash your hands to remove these pathogens. Your clothes can also carry the pathogens, so cleaning your clothing after any contact with ill plants will stop you from spreading the disease. Disinfect your tools and pots with a 10 percent bleach solution to remove any pathogens.

ORGANIC PEST CONTROL

Many people are interested in gardening organically, to avoid harmful chemicals making their way into their food. While many pesticides are harmless, there are other ways of pest control that don't involve these chemicals.

As mentioned before, companion planting is a great option for repelling pests. There is likely a plant out there that your particular pest hates, and planting that close to your vegetables will save them from being destroyed.

To identify any potential problem bugs or allies in your garden, an insect guide would be useful. You may actually have some of the good bugs eating your pests already. If not, good bugs such as ladybugs and praying mantises can be released into your garden to fight pests. While they are usually present in the environment already, purchasing some and releasing at the problem zone may get them started on your pests, and even create a continuing line of good bugs that reside in your garden and the surrounding area.

If you find pests on your plants, the first thing you can do is drop them into a container of soapy water. This may stop the pests before they become an infestation. If it's too late for hand removal, there are certified organic substances that can be used as natural pesticides.

Having a bird feeder or other bird attractor in your yard will draw them to your garden. While this is undesirable for some crops, the birds will eat the bugs from your garden and rid you of pests.

HOMEMADE ORGANIC PEST CONTROLS

While these homemade pest controls haven't been tested properly, they are an option if your plants are not too ill already.

SPRAY FOR POWDERY MILDEW AND BLACK SPOT

Ingredients:
2½ Tbs horticultural oil
3 Tbsp Baking Soda
One gallon of water

Spray the mixture onto affected plants. If the mildew persists, spray again.

SPRAY FOR BACTERIAL/FUNGAL DISEASES

Ingredients:
1 quart water
2 garlic cloves
1/8 tsp liquid soap

Begin by pureeing the garlic in your blender. Gradually add the water and continue blending for about 6 minutes. Strain out any larger pieces after blending, and mix in the liquid soap. Apply to any affected plants.

CABBAGE FAMILY PEST REPELLENT

Ingredients:
6 drops liquid soap

2 Tbsp red pepper

1 gallon water

Stir well and allow the mixture to sit out overnight before applying. Apply each week.

DEER DETERRENT

Mixture:
1 egg

1 gallon of water

Spray the mixture over your plants. Spray again once a week after initial application, more frequently if it has rained.

Other deer deterrents:

Sprinkle human hair around your garden. You can get bags of hair at barber shops, but this may get you some funny looks. Human urine repels deer also.

PROVEN ORGANIC PEST CONTROLS

These methods are more reliable than the other methods, as time has proven that they are effective.

Bacillius thuringienses, or BT, is a bacterium used to kill leaf-eating caterpillars, including the cabbage worm. BT is sold in the form of a soluble powder, which will be ingested by the unsuspecting pest, destroying its digestive system. Depending on which pest you want to kill, you may want to just sprinkle the powder, or spray directly onto the plants.

Diatomaceous earth is the fossilized remains of diatoms. This sediment is abrasive and is made primarily of silica. When it comes into contact with insects, it begins to absorb the moisture from their bodies, killing by dehydration. This can kill your good bugs, so caution should be used.

VEGETABLE & FRUIT HARVEST GUIDE

After your hard work during the growing season, you will finally be able to harvest your crop. Usually the main crop is in the fall, but depending on which plants you've chosen, the harvest time may vary. This section provides tips on when to harvest your plants, to ensure maximum flavor and storage.

APPLES

Photo courtesy of Wikimedia. Author: George Chernilevsky. Photograph taken: 24 August 2011. The photo is released into the public domain. This applies worldwide.

Depending on your variety, harvest time may be anytime from midsummer to late fall. To prevent the stems from accidentally coming loose, cup the apple in your palm, gently tilt it up, and turn the fruit. A ripe apple will separate easily from the tree using this method.

Another indication of ripeness is the seeds; they will turn dark brown when the apple is ripe. If the apple is mealy when you cut or bite it, it is too ripe.

Storage time can vary with variety, as some are better for storage than others. When stored at temperatures close to zero and high humidity, apples will last from a few weeks to 6 months. Root cellars are ideal for apple storage.

ASPARAGUS

Depending on how you planted the bed, you may have a light harvest after the asparagus has had a full growing season and is entering the second, but only harvest then if you started your bed from crowns. The third growing season is when the harvest really begins, as the plants will be well-established. Harvest a medium amount for 3 to 4 weeks during the third year. After the fourth year, you can harvest heavily for 6 weeks or more if desired.

When harvesting, select the spears that have grown to pencil size or thicker. If there are thinner spears, let them grow into ferns. The spears should be 6-8 inches tall, with firm, closed tips. Snap or cut the spears at about the ground level, taking care not to damage the plant's crown. Once the spears start to become too thin for harvest, stop your harvest.

Fresh asparagus is always best, but spears can be refrigerated for about a week. If refrigerating, set your asparagus in a tall container with 1-2 inches of water in it. If allowed to be wet, the spear tips will rot. If you need to preserve asparagus longer than a week, freeze the spears until you need them. Asparagus freezes well, so freezing is the best option for long-term preservation.

BEANS

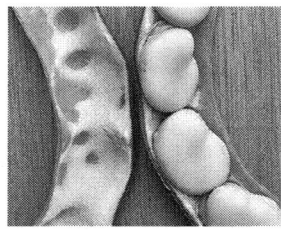

Fava beans. Photo courtesy of Wikimedia. Picture taken: 12 October 2011. Hohum at the English language Wikipedia, the copyright holder of this work, hereby publishes it under the following license:

With any of these bean varieties, harvest until the first frost. With shell and snap beans, you can keep the pods in plastic bags for 1 or 2 weeks in the refrigerator, or freeze the surplus.

SNAP BEANS

Snap beans are ripe when they are crisp and thick, with small, underdeveloped seeds. When ready to pick, the bean will snap when broken in half. If the seeds have developed, the beans are over mature. Gently pinch the pods off, keeping one hand on the stem and one on the pod. You can also use scissors if the beans are being stubborn. Always harvest the plants completely, as this keeps your plants producing.

SHELL BEANS

Pick shell beans when the pods have changed color and the beans are fully developed. The pods should be plump and firm. If left on the plant too long, the quality of the beans declines. These beans should be harvested every few days to keep plants producing. If desired, shell beans can be harvested like dried beans.

DRIED BEANS

Great Northern, Navy, Pinto, etc., come in both bush and pole varieties

These beans should only be harvested when the pods are dry and brown. The seeds should be hard and rattle in the pods. If the pods are fully dry, they will be easy to open. If the weather is too wet for the pods to dry completely, harvest the pods and hang them indoors until are fully dry. Place the dried beans in an airtight jar and store them in a cool, dry place. Putting a desiccant in the jar will keep the beans completely dry. Dry beans will store for about a year.

BROCCOLI

2 broccoli heads. Photo courtesy of Wikimedia. Taken in 2005. Author: David Monniaux

Broccoli heads that are ready to harvest are deep green, and compact. The buds have not yet opened. If the flowers start to open, harvest as soon as possible, as this will ruin the head. The head should be cut at a slant below the head, with 4-6 inches of stem.

With some varieties, removing the head will make the plant produce side shoots, which are also edible. Peel any stems that are to be eaten. The leaves are also edible, but a bit tough. Cook these in stews and soups.

Broccoli heads should be soaked in a salt water solution, 1 gallon of water to 1-2 tbsps of salt. There may be some cabbageworms in your head, and it would be a disaster if you cooked the broccoli with the worms inside. The salt water mixture will get rid of the worms in about 20-30 minutes. You can then cook the broccoli, or wrap it in plastic and refrigerate. If refrigerated, broccoli will keep for about a week. If you need to store broccoli for a longer time, it should be blanched and frozen.

CABBAGE

Image courtesy of Wikimedia. Permission is granted to copy, distribute and/or modify this document under the terms of the GNU Free Documentation License, Version 1.2 or any later version published by the Free Software Foundation; with no Invariant Sections, no Front-Cover Texts, and no Back-Cover Texts. A copy of the license is included in the section entitled GNU Free Documentation License.

Harvest cabbage when the head is firm and full. The morning is the best time to harvest, as the heads will be cool. Cut the head from the plant at the base, using a sharp knife. Remove the outer leaves. After this head has been removed, the plant may decide to send out more heads. These are usually small, but you may be able to get another large head out of one of these.

A root cellar is ideal for storing cabbage. They should be kept at almost freezing temperature and at about 90% humidity.

CARROTS

Image courtesy of Wikimedia Commons. This image is in the public domain because it contains materials that originally came from the Agricultural Research Service, the research agency of the United States Department of Agriculture.

Carrots are ready for harvest in 2-3 months, or when they grow large enough for use. The only way to tell if they are large enough is to pull a few up and check. Loosen the soil around the carrot with a fork, and gently lift them out of the ground. If they are large enough, brush off excess soil and twist off the tops. Watering beforehand will aid in pulling them from the ground.

You can leave your carrots in the ground if you don't feel like bringing them in; carrots will stay good in the ground unless the weather turns very hot. You do want to bring in your carrots before the ground freezes, but you can leave them until the first hard frost has passed.

Carrots can be stored in a root cellar for up to 4 months, but can be preserved by canning, freezing, or drying. If stored in a root cellar, they should be layered in moist sand or sawdust.

CAULIFLOWER

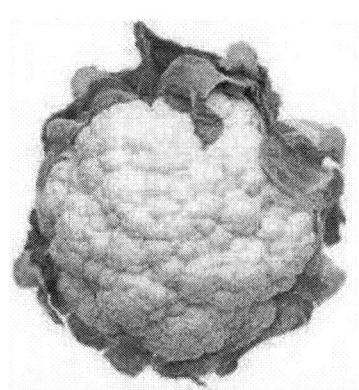

Cauliflower is ready to pick when the head is full, but before the curds separate. Cut the stem under the head, but leave a few leaves to protect the head. The head will bruise easily, so do this gently.

Like broccoli, cauliflower should be soaked in a salt water mixture of 1 to 2 tablespoons of salt to a gallon of water for 20-30 minutes before cooking or storing. This will drive out cabbageworms and make sure there are no nasty surprises.

If wrapped in plastic, cauliflower can be stored in the refrigerator, but it preserves best if blanched and frozen.

SWEET CORN

One a day foot item 20. Author: Darwin Bell. Taken: November 15th, 2006. Photo courtesy of Wikimedia Commons. This file is licensed under the Creative Commons Attribution 2.0 Generic license.

Sweet corn ears are ready for harvest when there is dark brown, soft silks, and the kernels are plump, tender, and produce milky liquid when pricked. If your kernels produce clear liquid, they are not ripe. If there is no liquid, the kernels are past their prime. Harvest corn in the late afternoon, by twisting the ear and pulling down.

As corn spoils quickly, you should use the corn immediately or preserve by freezing or canning. If you have a sugar-enhanced or super-sweet variety, you may be able to refrigerate the corn, but otherwise, it is best to freeze or can your surplus.

EGGPLANT

Solanum Melongena fruit on plant. Photo courtesy of Wikimedia Commons. Taken: 24 August 2012 Author: Joydeep. Joydeep, the copyright holder of this work, hereby publishes it under the following license: This file is licensed under the Creative Commons Attribution-Share Alike 3.0 Unported license.

Eggplant is best harvested when the seeds are barely visible and the skin is glossy and tight. The fruits will be about 4 to 5 inches long if a standard variety, and smaller for mini types. If the skin is dull, the eggplant is overripe and tough. Another sign that the eggplant is too ripe is if there are black seeds forming inside. The seeds should be just barely formed if the eggplant is ripe.

To harvest, cut the eggplant from the plant with about an inch of stem attached. Refrigerate.

LETTUCE

Close up of an iceberg lettuce field. Photo courtesy of Wikimedia. Taken: 4 August 2005. This file is licensed under the Creative Commons Attribution 1.0 Generic license.

LEAF LETTUCE (ROMAINE)

Lactuca sativa (Romaine variety). Location: Maui, Foodland Pukalani / 30 July 2007. Author: Forest & Kim Starr. Photograph courtesy of Wikimedia. This file is licensed under the Creative Commons Attribution 3.0 Unported license.

Leaf lettuce will mature about 40 days from seeding. Begin your harvest in the early morning when the leaves are about 4 to 5 inches long. YOu can either pick the outer leaves or cut the entire plant. If you choose to cut the full head, leave about an inch above the soil lone, as the plant will regrow the head in 3 to 5 weeks. If a hard frost is coming or your plants are starting to bolt, harvest immediately.

HEAD LETTUCE

Head and romaine lettuce mature slower than leaf lettuce, about 70 days from seeding, but this can be accelerated by using transplants. Transplants will mature about 20-35 days from planting. Harvest when heads are firm. The plant should be cut to the ground level when harvested. Lettuce will keep in the refrigerator for 1 to 2 weeks, but iceberg lettuce will keep longer. It's always a good idea to eat lettuce the same day as it is harvested, as it is crisp and likely still has the morning dew on it.

MELONS

MUSKMELONS (ALSO CALLED CANTALOUPE, ROCK MELON)

Muskmelon. Image courtesy of Wikimedia. Author: Seth Vidal | Taken: 5 August 2006. This image, which was originally posted to Flickr.com, was uploaded to Commons using Flickr upload bot on 16:39, 21 September 2008 (UTC) by Hohum. This file is licensed under the Creative Commons Attribution-Share Alike 2.0

Muskmelon that is picked when perfectly ripe is always the most flavorful. The plants will have given the fruit much more sugar in the last few days of ripening. This is why store-bought melons do not have as much flavor. It is simply impractical for the store to have vine-ripened fruit. Your melons will always have more flavor than those at the store.

Muskmelons will have a tan rind between the surface netting when ripe. The strongest sign that the melon is ripe is a crack forming on the stem near the melon. This crack will eliminate having to fight the plant to remove the melon. When the outer skin softens and is weak enough for birds and other wildlife to penetrate easily, the melon is too ripe and should be left to the wildlife.

HONEYDEWS

It is especially important to let honeydews ripen on the vine, as they are not any good if picked too soon. Make sure you keep track of when your variety matures, and do not ever pick before that date. If there was a cool spell during the season, leave the melons for a few more days. Even after picking, let the melons sit at room temperature for a few days, to ensure that they are completely ripe.

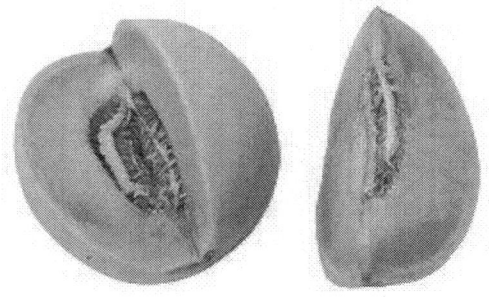

Organic honeydew melon. Picture courtesy of Wikimedia Commons. Author: Yotoen |Taken: 28 October 2009

WATERMELONS

Watermelons. Photo courtesy of Wikimedia Commons. Author: Steve Evans | Taken: 29 January 2005. This file is licensed under the Creative Commons Attribution 2.0 Generic license.

Ripe watermelons will have a deep sound when thumped, as well as a yellow underside. The tendril that connects it to the plant will also dry, signaling that the plant is done creating the fruit. Your melon will likely ripen some more after picking, so it should be stored at room temperature until fully ripe. After the melon is ripe, it can be refrigerated for several weeks, or cut into pieces and frozen.

BULB ONIONS AND GARLIC

Shallots, a smaller onion variant used for cooking. These were bought in the American Northeast. Photo courtesy of Wikimedia Commons. Author: Evan-Amos. Taken: 13 October 2011. This file is licensed under the Creative Commons Attribution-Share Alike 3.0 Unported license.

Garlic Bulbs. Picture courtesy of Wikimedia Commons. Author: JJHarrison. Taken: 15

BULB ONIONS

You can harvest onions before they are fully mature and use them as green onions, depending on your preference. If you want green onions, check a few bulbs to see whether they are big enough. If so, you can harvest.

When the tops of your onion plants turn yellow and fall over, your onions are mature. You can gently knock the tops over with the back of your rake to speed this process, but try not to snap the top off. Once the tops turn brown, you can lift the bulbs from the ground with a spading fork. Just brush off any soil; no washing is needed.

To prevent storage rot, let the bulbs dry in a warm, airy place out of the rain and sun for about a week. When the outer skins are dry and the tops are withered, cut the tops an inch from the bulb and bag them. Alternately, you can braid the tops together. Hang the onions in a cool, dry place.

GARLIC

Garlic is ready to harvest when the cloves have become segmented and easy to separate. Usually, the leaves will turn brown around that point. About 75% of the foliage should be brown before harvesting. Check a few bulbs to see if the cloves are segmented yet.

Avoid leaving garlic bulbs in the ground for extended periods of time. The outer skin will deteriorate and reduce storage time as well as the quality of the garlic.

Harvest bulbs using a pitchfork. The bulbs should be let dry in the sun for a few days, and then stored in a cool, dry place. As with onions, it is an option to braid the dried leaves to hang them, or to cut the foliage and put the bulbs into mesh bags. Either way, make sure to place your bulbs in a well-ventilated area.

SNOW AND SNAP PEAS

Snow Peas. Photograph courtesy of Wikimedia Commons. This work is in the public domain in the United States because it is a work prepared by an officer or employee of the United States Government as part of that person's official duties under the terms of Title 17, Chapter 1,

Section 105 of the US Code. Sugar snap peas. Photo courtesy of Wikimedia. Author: Brianga. Date taken: 10 January 2012. This file is licensed under the Creative Commons Attribution-Share Alike 3.0 Unported license.

The difference between snow and snap peas: with a snow pea pod, you can see the peas. With a snap pea, you will not be able to see the peas.

Wait 3 weeks after the pea plants begin to flower to harvest. The pods should be slightly bumpy. Any shriveled or discolored pods are overripe. The pods will be crispest in the early morning, and will stay fresh longer if harvested then. When harvesting, it is best to use scissors, as this will prevent accidental uprooting of the plant. Harvesting daily will promote more production from your plants.

Like corn, peas are best eaten immediately, or at least within one day. If you have surplus peas, freeze or can as soon as possible. You can also refrigerate peas for up to a week if needed. If you must refrigerate the peas, place them in a paper bag and then place the paper bag inside a plastic bag. This prevents the peas from sitting in water while keeping in enough moisture to keep them fresh.

PEARS

2 pears. Photo courtesy of Wikimedia Commons. Source: USDA, Image Number K5299-1. Author: Keith Weller This image or file is a work of a United States Department of Agriculture employee, taken or made as part of that person's official duties. As a work of the U.S. federal government, the image is in the public domain.

Unlike melons, pears are best harvested when they are still hard, and then allowed to ripen off the tree for some time. While you could wait until the fruit is soft to harvest, it will severely limit the storage time. When the green color lightens and the stem detaches from the spur with a light twist, the pear is ready to harvest. Once harvested, the pears should be allowed to soften and ripen more at about 65-70° F. Depending on your variety, the pears may be ripe in a few days or a few weeks.

To check your pears for ripeness, apply gentle pressure to pear, close to the stem. A ripe pear will yield to the pressure. Pears keep best when stored at near freezing temperature with high humidity. Each variety has a different storage length, so check how long your variety keeps.

PEPPERS

Capsicum – Chili. Image courtesy of Wikimedia Commons. Permission is granted to

Bell peppers hanging from plant. Photograph courtesy of Wikimedia Commons. Author: الـ بـلغم فـ ارس | Taken 26 May 2013. This file is licensed under the Creative Commons Attribution-Share Alike 3.0 Unported license.

Peppers can be harvested as soon as they reach the desired size. Harvest continuously after the first harvest to keep your plants productive. Depending on your intended use, you may choose to pick your peppers while green, or let them ripen.

Bell peppers should be cut from the plant with ½ inch of stem still attached. A sharp knife or pair of pruning shears would be handy for this. Some peppers will come off with the stem still attached without cutting, but if you have trouble getting them off the plant, switch to cutting, as this will prevent damage to the plant.

If the peppers are left out in a warm room, they will continue to ripen. Refrigerate your peppers to keep them from over-ripening. Thick-walled peppers can be stored in plastic bags and refrigerated for up to 2 weeks. Peppers can also be frozen or pickled, if desired. Before freezing, wash the peppers, cut them into strips, and blanch them for 30 seconds in boiling water.

Small peppers will start drying as soon as they are removed from the plant. Lay out the peppers in a single layer in a warm place, until they are almost crisp. They can then be stored in airtight jars.

POTATOES

Potato with sprouts, Russet variety. Photograph courtesy of Wikimedia Commons. Author: ZooFari | Taken: 27 December 2009. This

A sign that your potatoes are becoming mature is the plant's stems and leaves. They will begin to turn brown when the potatoes start to mature. However, you can simply harvest the potatoes whenever they become large enough for your use. If you intend to store your potatoes, be careful of potatoes with thin skins. The best potatoes for storage will have tough skins that do not peel off easily with a finger.

If you have some potatoes with thin skins, those would be best used immediately rather than stored. Curing your potatoes will make them store better. To cure the potatoes, place them in a single layer on newspapers at about 50-60° F for two weeks. After curing, they should be stored at about 40° F. Wherever you store your potatoes, ensure there is no light in the area. The potatoes will turn green if allowed to sit in the light.

At harvest time, you may be able to just pull up the potato plants if your soil is loose enough. Even if you can pull the plant, search the soil for stray potatoes. If your soil isn't loose enough to pull the plants, use a pitchfork to pull the potatoes up. The potatoes should be left outside for an hour or two to dry.

PUMPKINS AND OTHER SQUASH

Pumpkins and squashes. Photograph courtesy of Wikimedia Commons. Author: George Chernilevsky | Taken: 11 September 2011. I, the copyright holder of this work, release this work into the public domain. This applies worldwide. In some countries this may not be legally possible; if so: I grant anyone the right to use this work for any purpose, without any conditions, unless such conditions are required by law.

PUMPKINS AND WINTER SQUASH

Harvest pumpkins and winter squash when the rind is hard enough to resist puncturing with a fingernail, or wait until the plants begin to die back. When handling any kind of pumpkin, try not to pick it up by the stem because if the stem gets broken off, this is a weak spot for decay. Pumpkins and winter squash are ready to harvest when their rinds are hard enough to resist being cut with a fingernail. Another sign of maturity is when the plant stems begin to die back.

Avoid handling pumpkins by the stems, as a broken stem will likely lead to a decay spot. Squash should be spread out in a single layer if possible, but if they must be stacked, avoid stacking more than 2 high. This will prevent rot.

Winter squash and pumpkins should be cured in a 75 to 80° F, dry, well ventilated are for 10 to 12 days. Once the fruits are cured, dip them in a solution of 1 part bleach to 10 parts water. This will kill fungi and bacteria, allowing longer storage.

Allow them to air dry and them move them to a cool, dark, dry, and well ventilated storage area. The temperature should be within 50-55° F. Damp root cellars are not ideal for pumpkins and winter squash, as the moisture will cause rot.

SUMMER SQUASH AND ZUCCHIN

Summer squash. Photo courtesy of Wikimedia Commons. Author: Forest and Kim Starr. Taken: 22 August 2011 This file is licensed under the Creative Commons Attribution 2.0 Generic license.

Summer squash should be harvested when immature and tender. Pick summer squash when the squash are 6 to 8 inches long, and about 2 inches in diameter. Patty pan and scallop squash should be harvested when 3 or 4 inches in diameter. Harvest all squashes so the plants continue to produce. When harvesting, cut fruits with 1 inch of stem attached. Refrigeration is a good storage method for summer squash.

TOMATOES

Tomato fruits. Image courtesy of Wikipedia Commons. Author: H. Zell. Taken: 29 July 2009. Permission is granted to copy, distribute and/or modify this document under the terms of the GNU Free Documentation License, Version 1.2 or any later version published by the Free Software Foundation; with no Invariant Sections, no Front-Cover Texts, and no Back-Cover Texts. A copy of the license is included in the section entitled GNU Free Documentation License.

It's easy to tell when tomatoes are ripe; they turn bright red (or with some varieties, purple or another color). Let your tomatoes vine ripen and pick when firm and fully colored. Some varieties will drop their fruits as they ripen. These are perfectly fine, but avoid growing those varieties vertically.

Store at room temperature, never store tomatoes in the refrigerator. When chilled, tomatoes lose their flavor. This is the reason why fresh tomatoes from your garden taste better than the tomatoes at the grocery store; grocery store tomatoes are always refrigerated.

CONCLUSION

It takes a lot of work to tend a garden, but it is certainly worth the effort. The money you can save from having your own tomatoes, watermelon, lettuce, fruits, and berries, can be worth whatever time and effort that you have to expend. Think of all of that money that you would have spent at the grocery supermarket, and now you have a lot of what you need right there in your own garden. You also don't have to worry about what pesticides that have been put on them (which you ultimately consume) because you oversaw them the entire time.

It really makes sense on a lot of levels to grow your own garden. I hope you learned something that will help you from reading this eBook. And remember that you can always experiment on your own. Thanks for reading, and good luck with your garden!

ABOUT THE AUTHOR

Brought up on a long-established Texas farm, James McAllen helped his dad and grandfather till the ground and plant their annual vegetable gardens the traditional way. Having earned a BS in Horticulture from Texas A&M University, James saved his money and bought a farm of his own, but he didn't know how he wanted to garden until he researched the seven best-known methods. Gardening – Seven Best Methods is James' first book on gardening. This book is his second.

Shown here with his faithful dog, Sandy, James' plans for a third book, Urban Homesteading, Your Guide to Self-Sufficiency: Why You Should Start NOW! coming out on or before May, 2016

MORE BOOKS FROM DELL
PUBLISHING PRESS

Herbal Remedies

Your Ultimate Guide to Relieve Stress, Anxiety, Pain, Skin Conditions and for Weight Loss

Master Herbalist Grace McAllen

FOR *BEGINNERS AND INTERMEDIATES*

GLUTEN FREE COOKBOOK FOR BUSY MOMS

BOOK 2

50 NUTRITIOUS RECIPES TO SAVE MOMS TIME AND MONEY

HELEN MARIE

Made in the USA
Lexington, KY
14 April 2017